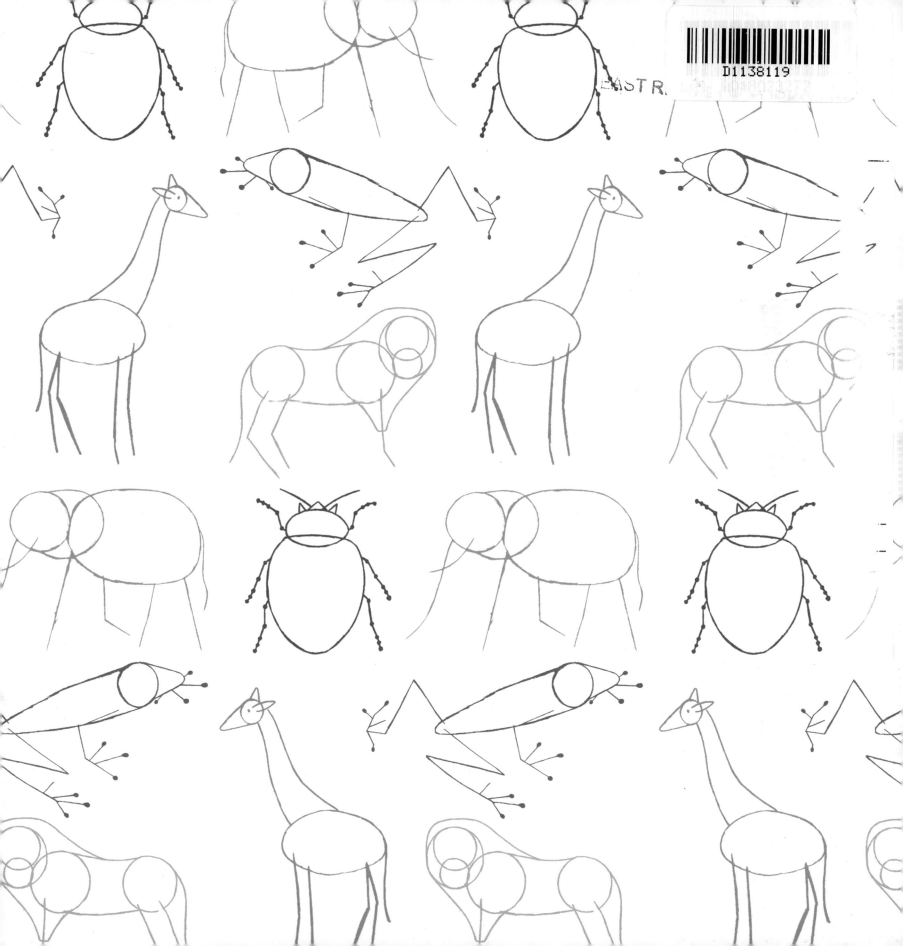

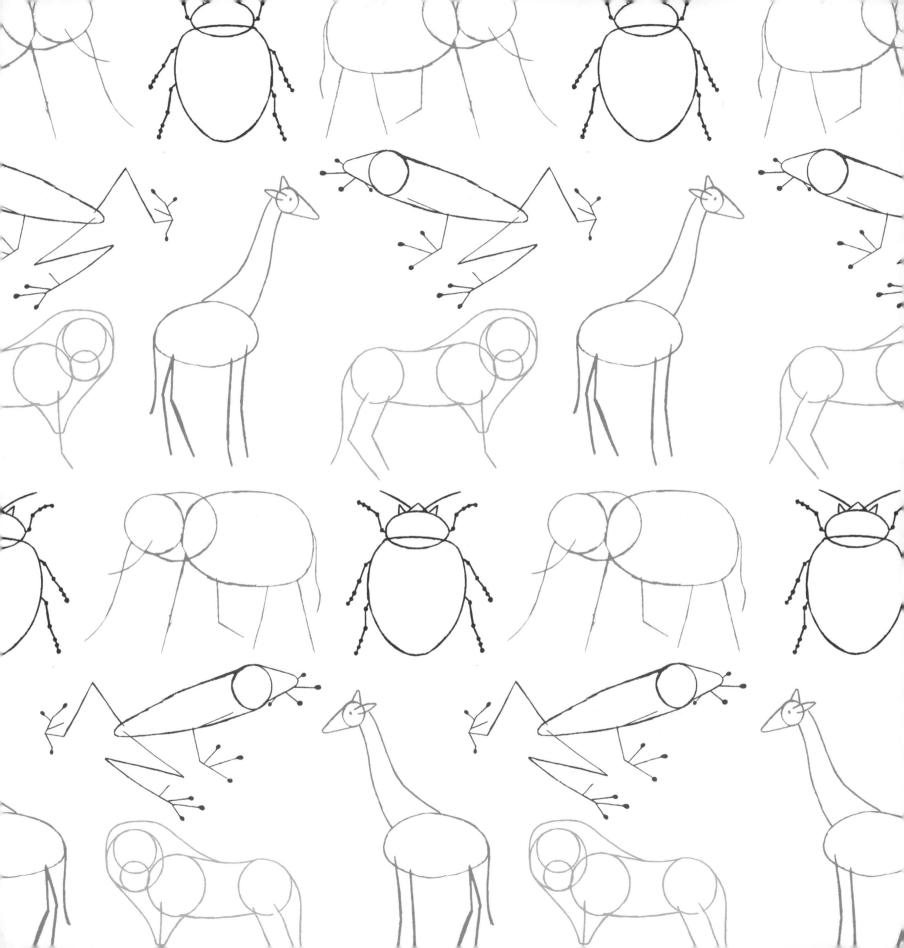

This book belongs to:

....

....

GRAFFEG

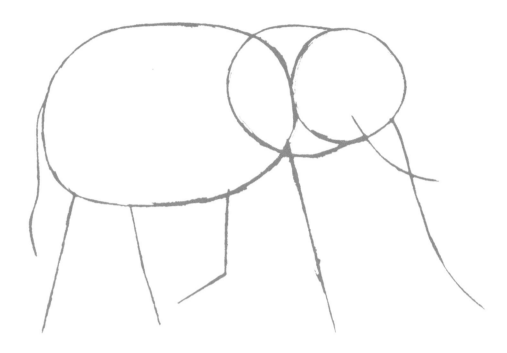

Animal Surprises: How to Draw
published by Graffeg 2017
© Copyright Graffeg 2017
ISBN 9781912050567

Text © 2017 Nicola Davies.
Illustrations © 2017 Abbie Cameron.
Designed and produced by Graffeg
www.graffeg.com

Graffeg Limited, 24 Stradey Park Business
Centre, Mwrwg Road, Llangennech, Llanelli,
Carmarthenshire SA14 8YP Wales UK
Tel 01554 824000 www.graffeg.com

Graffeg are hereby identified as the authors of
this work in accordance with section 77 of the
Copyrights, Designs and Patents Act 1988.

A CIP Catalogue record for this book is available
from the British Library.

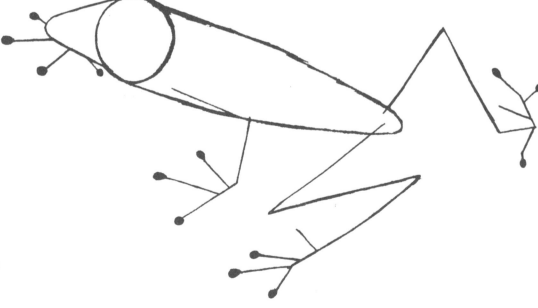

ANIMAL SURPRISES

How to Draw

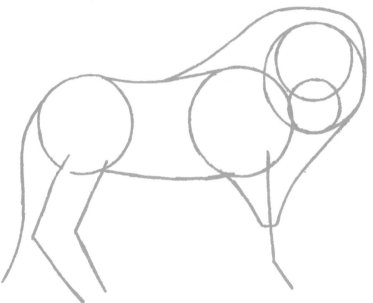

Written by
Nicola Davies

Illustrated by
Abbie Cameron

Animals come in all sizes, shapes and colours, from microbes too teeny to see to whales as big as a bus, from elephants grey as a cloud to frogs like mini rainbows. There are so many different kinds that scientists haven't even counted them all yet, and new kinds are being found all the time. Drawing the animals in this book will help you to notice the things that make each one special. Who knows, one day, you could be a scientist and discover a new animal that no one has ever found or noticed before.

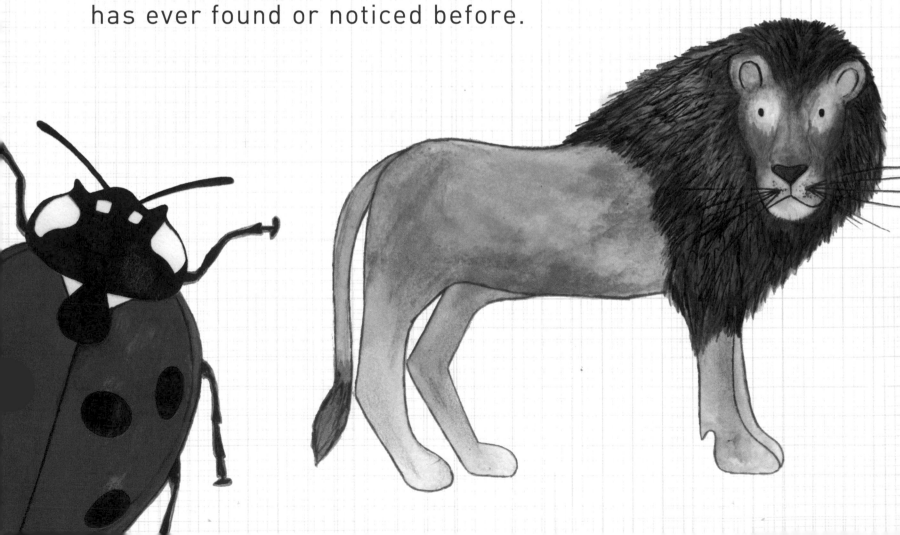

Learn to draw some of the most amazing animals on the planet following the step-by-step instructions in this book.

Here are some drawing materials you can use:

✓
- ☐ Drawing pad
- ☐ Felt pens
- ☐ Colour pencils
- ☐ Crayons
- ☐ Drawing pencil
- ☐ Rubber
- ☐ Sharpener

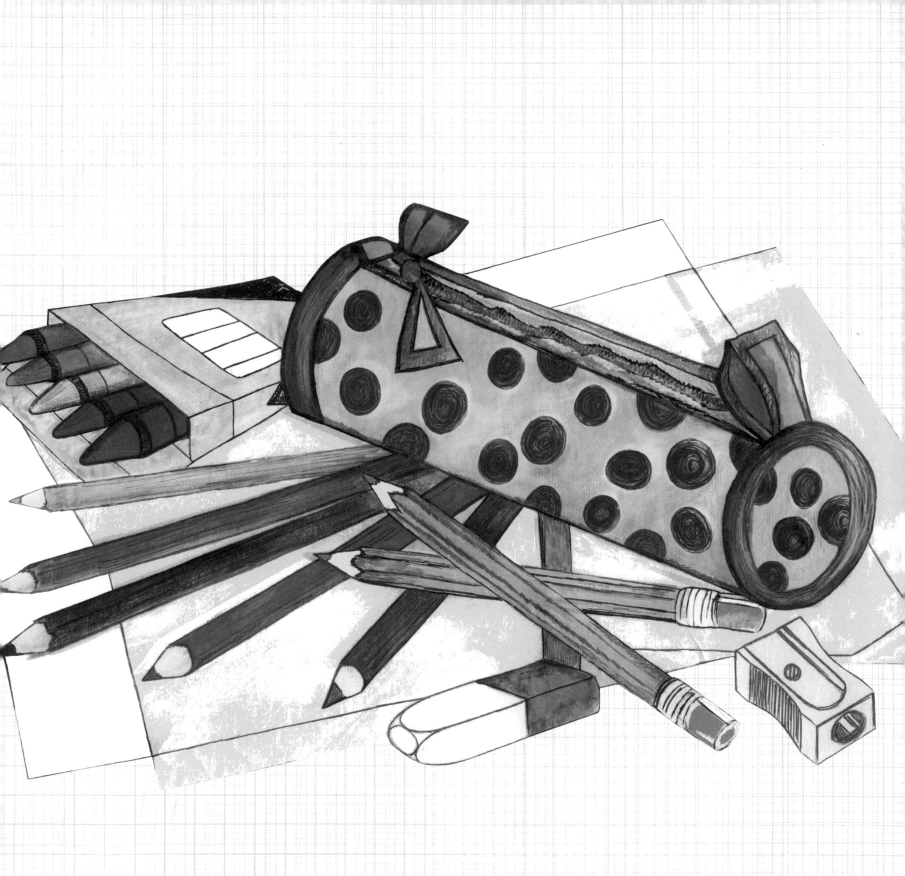

How to Draw a Lion

Step 1

Draw two circles side by side. The right-hand circle should be slightly larger.

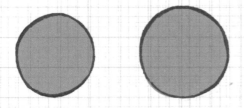

Step 2

Join them together and add another overlapping circle for the head.

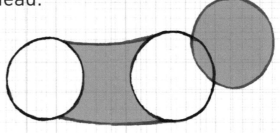

Step 3

Draw two curved lines, one around the top of the head and one around the bottom for the mane and front legs.

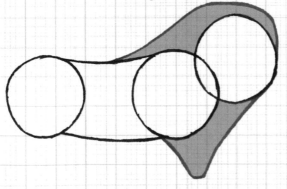

Step 4

Draw three angled lines for the legs, and a curved line at the back for the tail.

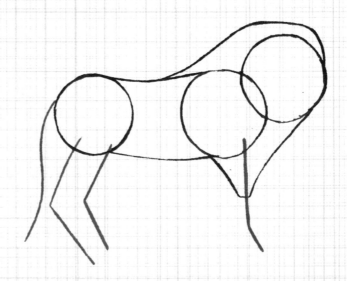

Step 5

Draw in the outline of the lion's legs, paws and tail.

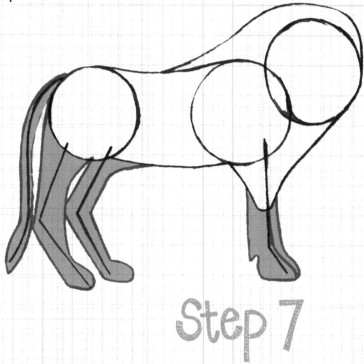

Step 6

Add two overlapping circles to the head for the face and draw in the ears, nose and mouth.

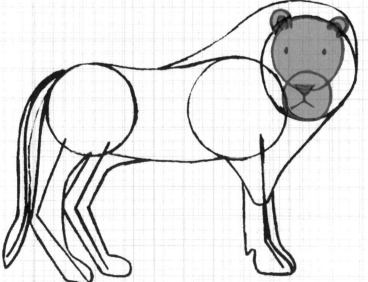

Step 7

Add more details to the face and mane.

Step 8

Rub out the guide-lines and colour in your lion. Unlike other big cats the lion doesn't have spots or stripes, but you can colour in their bright mane and tail.

Did you know?

Lions are powerful hunters, but unlike other big cats they live in family groups called prides. Pride survival depends on having a good territory, with water to drink and to attract prey like zebra or wildebeest. It's the male lion's job to defend the family territory. So although all lions are tawny coloured to be camouflaged against the sun-dried grass of their home, males also have a mane. This makes them look big and tough and, together with a loud roar, helps to keep strangers away.

How to Draw an Elephant

Step 1

Draw one large oval.

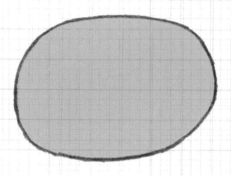

Step 2

Draw a circle touching the right hand side of the oval.

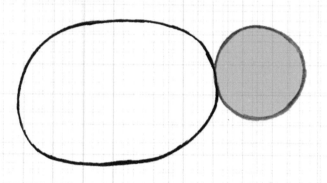

Step 3

Add a curved shape to the left side of the circle for the elephant's ear.

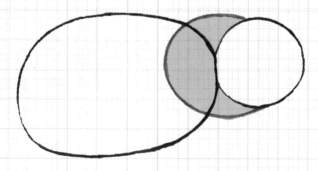

Step 4

For the legs, draw four lines coming down from the body.

Step 5

Draw in lines for the tail, tusks and trunk.

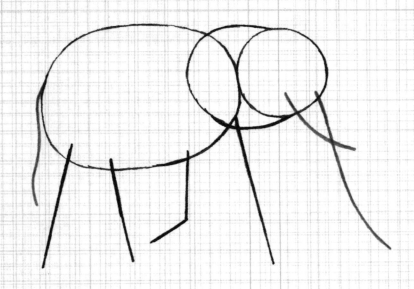

Step 6

Add some more detail to the elephant's face, drawing around the ear and trunk.

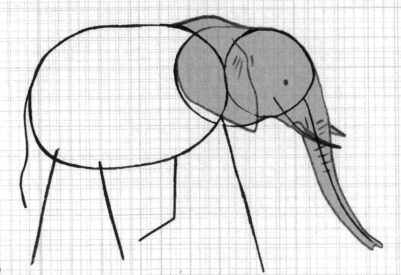

Step 7

Fill in the elephant's legs and body by drawing around your outline, making sure to add in the toes and tail.

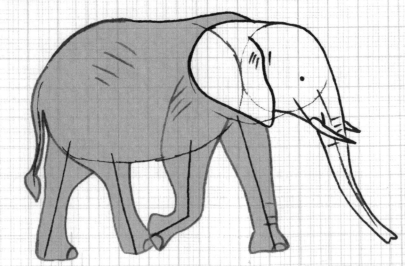

Step 8

Rub out the guide-lines and colour the elephant grey, adding some shadow around the ear and along the trunk.

Did you Know?

Elephants are the biggest animals on land. There are two different kinds, African and Indian. This picture shows the African elephant. Both use their trunks for lots of jobs, from cuddling their babies to ripping a tree apart for food. They are long-lived, highly intelligent and very sociable. Herds are led by the oldest female, or matriarch. All the elephants in the group rely on their long memory of where to find the best food and sources of water in a drought.

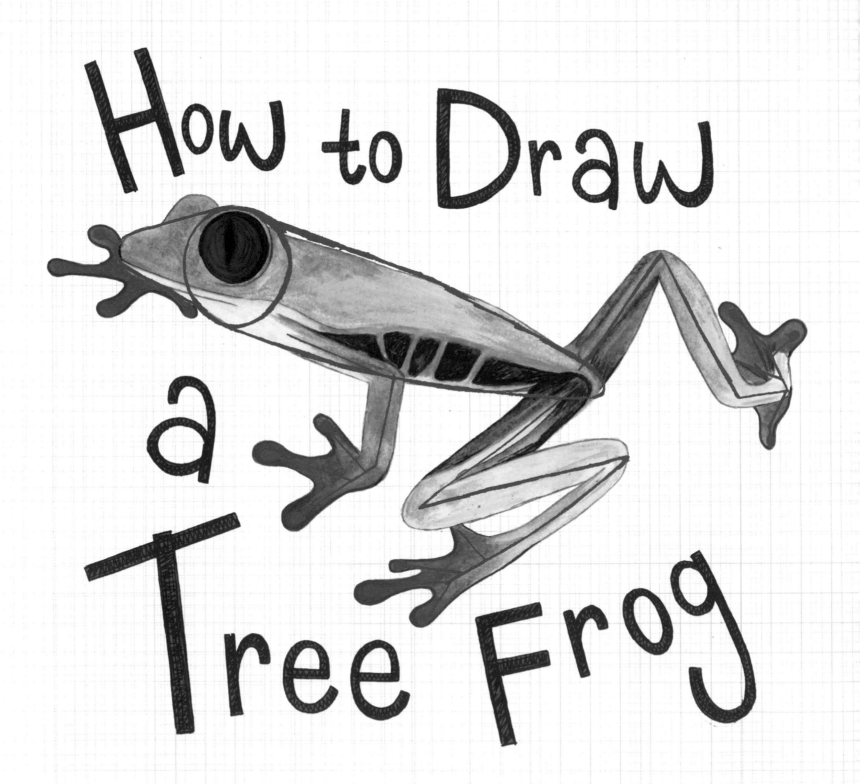

How to Draw a Tree Frog

Step 1

Draw a circle.

Step 2

Add a long, pointy shape to the right hand side of the circle.

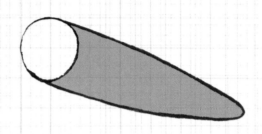

Step 3

Draw a blunt, rounded triangle to the left-hand side of the circle.

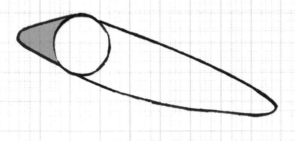

Step 4

Give your frog legs and feet using long, straight lines. Add in its little round toes.

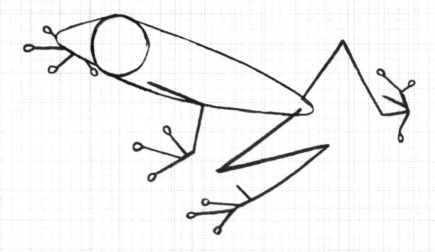

Step 5

Draw around the lines to create the frog's outline. Remember to give it webbed feet.

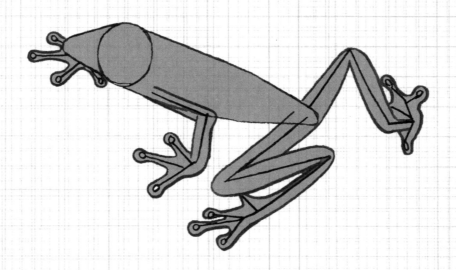

Step 6

Add some more detail to the frog's face by drawing a big, round eye.

Step 7

Give your frog a stripy belly. Extend the top line of its belly all the way along the bottom of its head up to its nose.

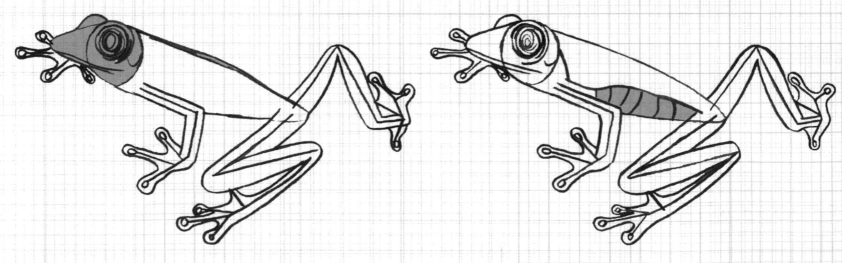

Step 8

Rub out the guildelines and colour your tree frog. The tree frog uses its bright colours to scare off predators.

Did you know?

Frogs are amphibians. Adults need to keep their skin moist, and their eggs and tadpoles need water to grow into frogs. In spite of this, frogs have done well and there are more than 4000 different kinds. They are especially fond of tropical rainforests, and, at night, jungles are alive with the calls of many different frogs. This red-eyed tree frog from South America has sticky pads on its toes to help it cling to wet leaves in the trees.

How to Draw a Giraffe

Step 1

Draw an egg shape.

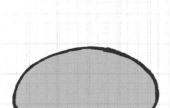

Step 2

Draw a small circle above the egg shape for the head.

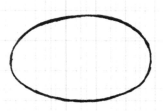

Step 3

Draw in three triangles for the giraffe's nose, 'horns' and ears.

Step 4

Connect the head to the body with two curved lines.

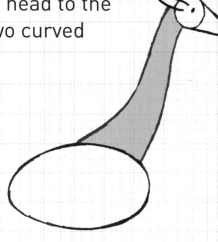

23

Step 5

Draw four straight lines for the legs and one for the tail. Put a slight bend in the lines for the back legs.

Step 6

Using the outline, fully draw in the shape of the legs and body. Add detail to the tail.

Step 7

Draw in lots of wonky spots to give the giraffe his distinctive pattern. Draw a squiggly line down the back of the neck.

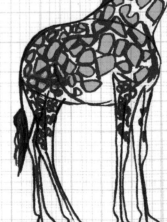

Step 8

Rub out the guide-lines and colour in the giraffe's yellow and brown pattern.

Did you Know?

Giraffes are the living skyscrapers of the African plains. Although their necks have the same number of bones as ours, they are very large and lift their heads higher than a double-decker bus. This means they can eat leaves from trees that other animals can't reach, but it creates a problem; giraffe hearts must work extra hard to pump blood up to their heads. It's a long way, so giraffes have very high blood pressure, twice as high as ours.

How to Draw a Ladybird

Step 1

Draw an oval with a flat top.

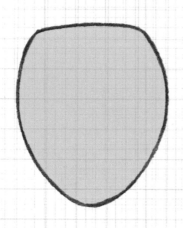

Step 2

Overlap another smaller oval at the top to make the head.

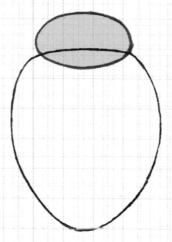

Step 3

For the pincers and antennae, draw two triangles and a small semicircle with long lines pointing out to the sides.

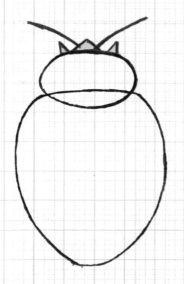

Step 4

Draw two legs coming from either side of the ladybird's head, two from its middle and two from lower down its body.

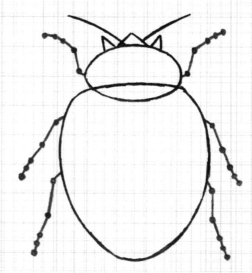

Step 5

Add to your outline by drawing in the full shape of the legs and antennae.

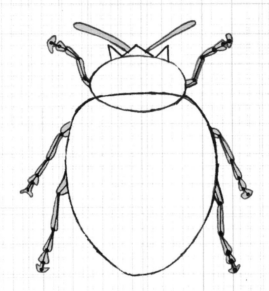

Step 6

Add the ladybird's eyes and facial markings.

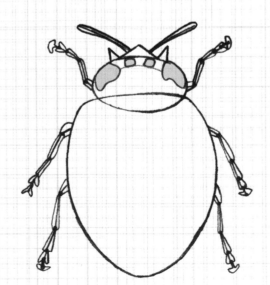

Step 7

Add detail to the ladybird's back. Ladybird's spots are symmetrical, so try to draw its spots the same on both sides.

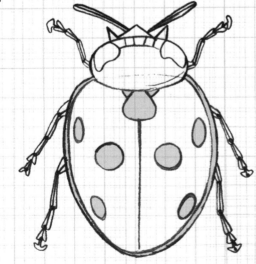

Step 8

Rub out the guidelines and colour in the lady-bird's signature black and red pattern.

Did you Know?

Ladybirds are beetles. They may look cute, but they are fierce little predators. Both the adults and their larvae eat aphids and a single ladybird can munch its way through 50 in a day! And when they have finished eating they lift their shiny wing cases to spread their wings and fly off. There are 46 different kinds in the UK, with different numbers and colours of spots, and around 5000 across the world.

Nicola Davies

Nicola is an award-winning author, whose many books for children include *The Promise* (Green Earth Book Award 2015, CILIP Kate Greenaway Shortlist 2015), *Tiny* (AAAS Subaru Prize 2015), *A First Book of Nature*, *Whale Boy* (Blue Peter Award Shortlist 2014), and the *Heroes of the Wild* series (Portsmouth Book Prize 2014). Nicola graduated in Zoology, studied whales and bats and then worked for the BBC Natural History Unit. Underlying all Nicola's writing is the belief that a relationship with nature is essential to every human being, and that now, more than ever, we need to renew that relationship. Nicola's children's books from Graffeg include *The Pond*, *Perfect* (CILIP Kate Greenaway Longlist 2017), the *Shadows and Light* series, *Animal Surprises*, *The Word Bird* and *Into the Blue*.

Abbie Cameron

Abbie Cameron was raised on the farmlands of the West Country. Surrounded by nature, she developed a love and appreciation for all creatures great and small. Abbie studied Illustration at University of Wales Trinity Saint David, where she first met Nicola Davies. Her style is playful and inventive, sharing some of the tongue-in-cheek attitude and doodle-like style of other contemporary British illustrators. Abbie employs the use of bright colours and texture, whilst playing with scale, composition and open space. Her other books include *Animal Surprises* (The Klaus Flugge Prize for the Most Exciting Newcomer to Picture Book Illustration Longlist 2017), *The Word Bird* and *Into the Blue*. Abbie was also highly commended for the Penguin Random House Design Awards 2014.

Rhyming Book Series

Discover the delights of nature with zoologist and top children's author Nicola Davies. Follow the young adventurer as she treks through the jungle in *Animal Surprises*, dives deep down into the sea in *Into the Blue* and climbs up high into the trees in *The Word Bird*. All three rhyming books are fully illustrated in colour by Abbie Cameron.

Titles in the series:
- **Animal Surprises**
- **The Word Bird**
- **Into the Blue**
- **The Secret of the Egg**
- **Invertebrates are Cool**
- **The Versatile Reptile**

How to Draw Series

In these step-by-step how to draw books, Abbie Cameron teaches children how to draw their favourite animals from the rhyming book series, alongside informative text from Nicola Davies about each species.

Titles in the series:
- **Animal Surprises: How to Draw**
- **The Word Bird: How to Draw**
- **Into the Blue: How to Draw**

Visit **www.graffeg.com/howtodraw** to watch Abbie drawing some of the animals from the series with step-by-step instructions.

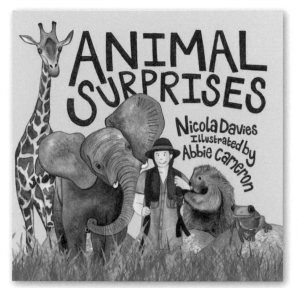

Animal Surprises
ISBN 9781910862445

The Word Bird
ISBN 9781910862438

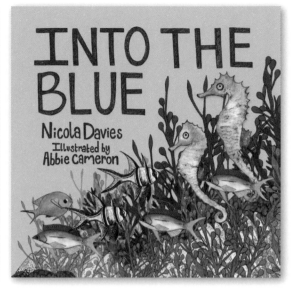

Into the Blue
ISBN 9781910862452

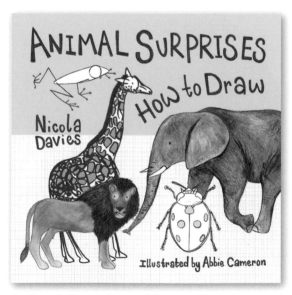

Animal Surprises: How to Draw
ISBN 9781912050567

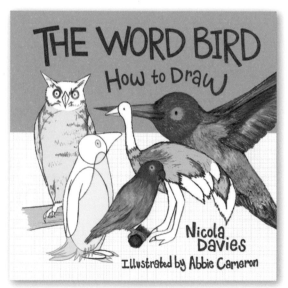

The Word Bird: How to Draw
ISBN 9781912050574

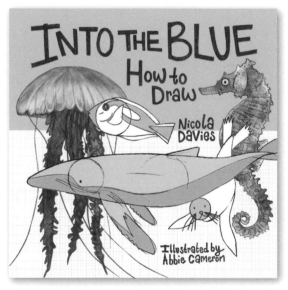

Into the Blue: How to Draw
ISBN 9781912050550

GRAFFEG
www.graffeg.com

Drawing Pages

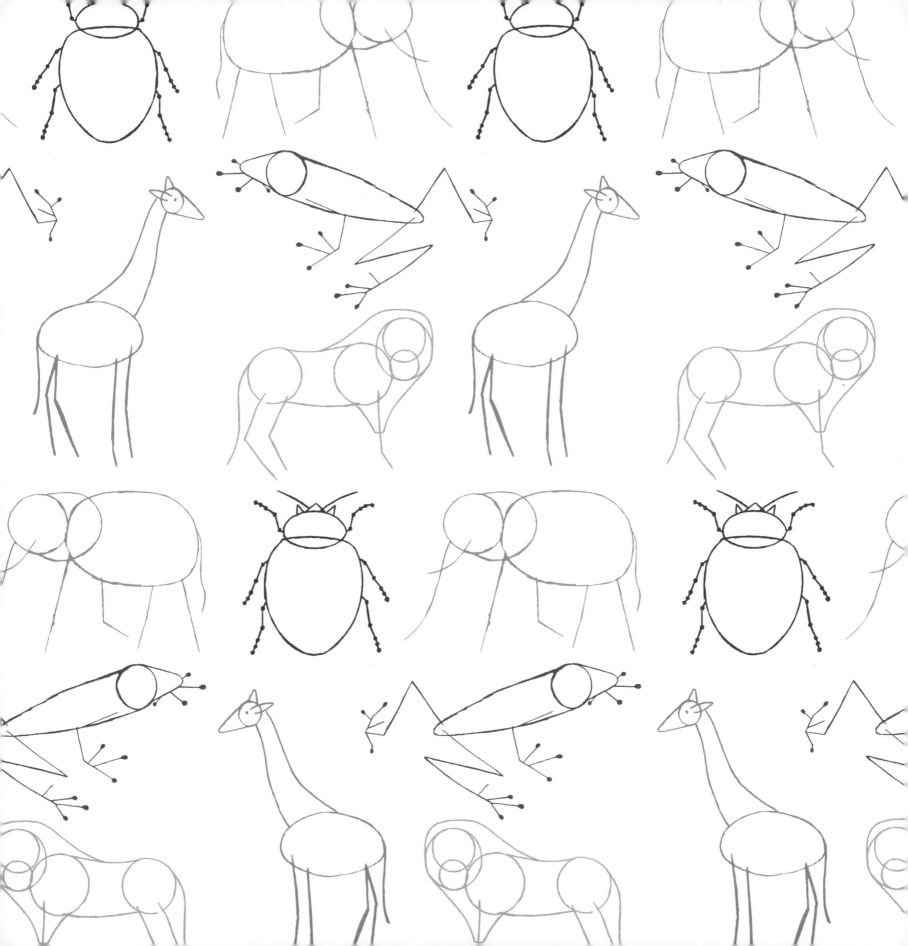

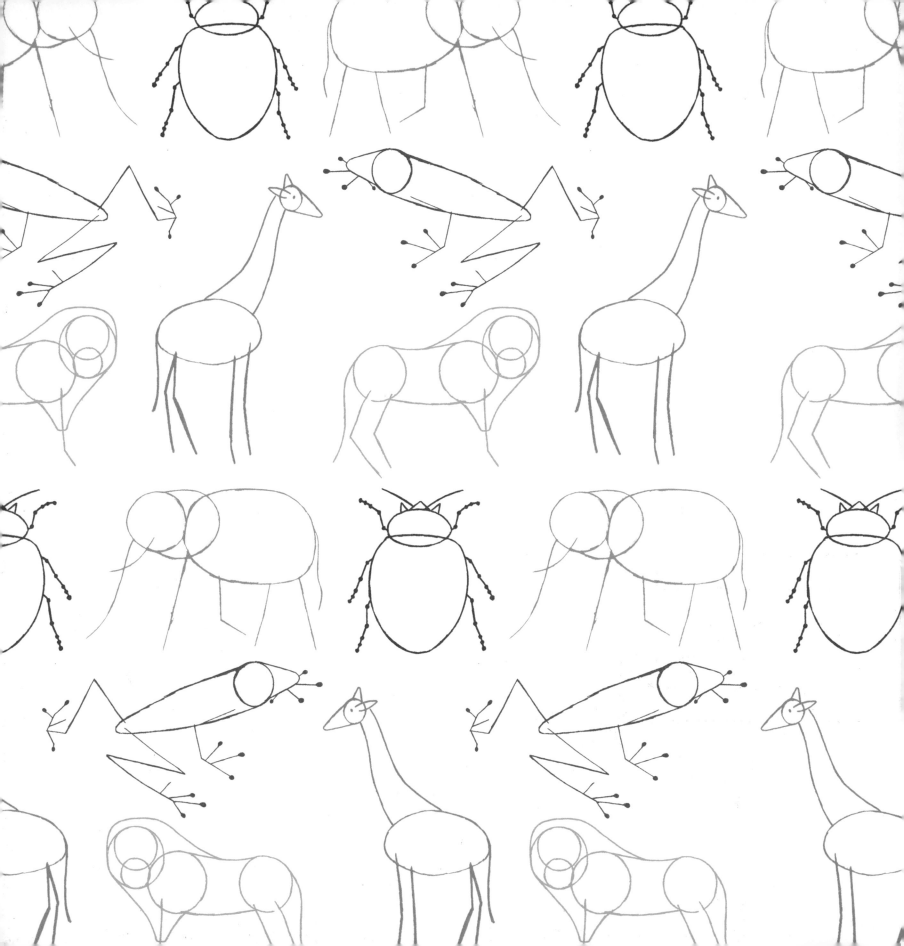